Read and Experiment

Experiments
with
MATERIALS

Isabel Thomas

heinemann
raintree

Edited by Holly Beaumont and Mandy Robbins
Designed by Steve Mead
Picture research by Jo Miller
Production by Helen McCreath
Originated by Capstone Global Library Ltd
Printed and bound in the USA by Corporate Graphics

19 18 17 16 15
10 9 8 7 6 5 4 3 2 1

Library of Congress Cataloging-in-Publication Data
Experiments with materials / Isabel Thomas.
    pages cm.—(Read and experiment)
  Summary: "Read and Experiment is an engaging series,
introducing children to scientific concepts. Explore the world
of materials with clear text, real-world examples and fun, safe
step-by-step experiments. This book brings materials science
to life, explaining the concepts and encouraging children to
be hands-on scientists."—Provided by publisher.
  Includes bibliographical references and index.
  ISBN 978-1-4109-7923-0 (hb)—ISBN 978-1-4109-7929-2 (pb)—
ISBN 978-1-4109-7940-7 (ebook) 1. Materials—Properties—
Experiments—Juvenile literature. 2. Matter—Properties—
Experiments—Juvenile literature. 3. Science projects—
Juvenile literature. I. Title.

TA403.2.T46 2016
530.4078—dc23   2014041770

This book has been officially leveled by using the F&P Text
Level Gradient™ Leveling System.

Acknowledgements
We would like to thank the following for permission to re-
produce photographs: Getty Images: National Geographic/
James L. Amos, 17; Glow Images: ImageSource, cover (bot-
tom), 15 (bottom); Science Source: Colin Cuthbert, 7 (bottom);
Shutterstock: Africa Studio, 23 (top), Dean Fikar, 23 (bottom),
Madlen, 10, michaeljung, 5, 28 (top), Pavel L Photo and Video,
7 (top), TRIG, 16

All other photographs were created at Capstone Studio by
Karon Dubke.

We would like to thank Patrick O'Mahony for his invaluable
help in the preparation of this book.

Every effort has been made to contact copyright holders
of material reproduced in this book. Any omissions will be
rectified in subsequent printings if notice is given to the
publisher.

All the internet addresses (URLs) given in this book were valid
at the time of going to press. However, due to the dynamic
nature of the internet, some addresses may have changed, or
sites may have changed or ceased to exist since publication.
While the author and publisher regret any inconvenience this
may cause readers, no responsibility for any such changes can
be accepted by either the author or the publisher.

The publisher and author disclaim, to the maximum extent
possible, all liability for any accidents, injuries, or losses that
may occur as a result of the information or instructions in
this book.

Safety Instructions for Adult Helper
The experiments in this book should be planned and carried out with adult supervision. Certain steps should
only be carried out by an adult—these are indicated in the text. Always follow the instructions carefully.

The materials used in these experiments are safe to handle, unless you have a specific allergy (e.g. egg,
page 11). Some everyday materials, such as vinegar, may irritate sensitive eyes or skin. It is recommended
to wear eye protection when mixing materials. Wash your hands after each experiment. Never eat or drink
anything used in your experiments or use eating utensils for experiments.

Contents

Some words are shown in bold, **like this**. You can find out what they mean by looking in the glossary.

Why Experiment?

Why can't we see the salt in the sea? Does hot chocolate *have* to be made with hot water?

Scientists ask questions like these. They work out the answers using **scientific inquiry**—and the really fun part is the **experiments**!

You can be a scientist by asking questions about the world and using experiments to help find the answers.

Follow these steps to work like a scientist:

Ask a question.

Come up with an idea to test.

Plan an experiment.

What will you change?
What will you keep the same?
What will you measure?

Make a **prediction**.

Observe carefully.

Work out what the results mean.

Answer the question!

An experiment is a test that has been carefully planned to answer a question.

The experiments in this book will help you to find out more about **materials** and what happens when you mix different materials together.

IS IT A FAIR TEST?

Most experiments involve changing something to see what happens. Make sure you only change one **variable** at a time. Then you will know that the variable you are testing is what made the difference. This is called a fair test.

WARNING! Ask an adult to help you plan and carry out each experiment. Follow the instructions carefully. If you see these signs, you will need to take extra care or ask for adult help.

ADULT HELP

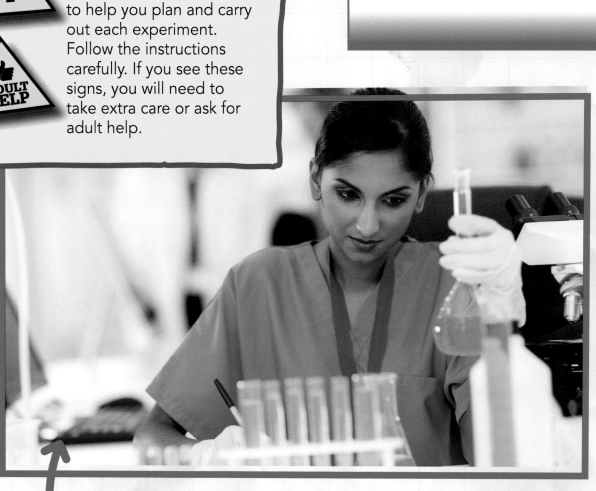

Get your eyes, ears, nose, and hands ready! You'll need to observe your experiments carefully and record what you see, hear, smell, and feel.

What Are Materials?

Everything you can see, touch, smell, or breathe in is made of "stuff." To describe that "stuff," scientists use the word **materials**.

Most materials, such as air, rocks, and cotton, are found in nature. People can invent new materials by mixing and changing natural materials. Plastic and concrete are **synthetic** materials.

SEE THE SCIENCE ⤵

Pick two materials and compare their **properties**. Are the materials **transparent** or **opaque**? Do they take in water or are they waterproof? Are they hard or soft? How many other properties can you think of?

Describing Materials

When we describe materials, we often talk about the way they look or behave in different situations. "Waterproof," "bouncy," "shiny," and "see-through" are all properties.

Right for the Job

Every material has a set of properties that makes it useful for certain jobs—and completely useless for others!

What would happen if you swapped the materials used for each part of this toy? Would it still fly?

REAL WORLD SCIENCE

Materials scientists study the properties of materials. They use their findings to sort materials into groups. They also design new materials with the right combination of properties for certain tasks.

Knee Pads

Knowing about properties helps us choose the right material for a job. This **experiment** will help you find the best fabric to protect your knees when you're riding a scooter or skateboarding.

Equipment

- 4 x 6-inch (10 x 15-centimeter) strips of different fabrics (e.g. denim, polyester, cotton, jersey, wool, nylon, fleece, canvas)
- Cork sanding block
- Tack
- Small wooden block
- Rough sandpaper

Predict: Which fabric will be the toughest? Which will be the weakest?

Method

1. Stretch a piece of fabric tightly around the sanding block, pinning it in place on the backside.

2 Cut a piece of sandpaper and wrap it around the small wooden block. Rub it along the fabric from top to bottom.

3 Keep rubbing in the same way, counting as you go. How many rubs until you can see the cork through the fabric? Record your result.

4 Repeat these steps with the other pieces of fabric. Record your results in a table, like the one below. Do your results match your prediction?

Fabric	Number of times rubbed with sandpaper before a hole appeared

 IS IT A FAIR TEST?

Rubbing wears the sandpaper down, as well as the fabric. To make it a fair test, use a new piece of sandpaper each time.

Conclusion

The toughest fabric is the one that withstood the highest number of rubs. This would be the best type of fabric to wear for protecting your knees when riding a scooter or skateboarding.

What Is a Mixture?

Another set of **properties** describes how **materials** behave when you mix them with other materials. A **mixture** is made up of two or more materials. The materials in a mixture have not changed—they are just jumbled up together.

This is a mixture of different types of candies.

Mixtures and Solutions

If you mix a spoonful of mud into a jar of water, pieces of mud spread through the water, turning it brown. If you mix salt with water (like in the sea), the salt seems to vanish and the water still looks clear. Where does the salt go?

Salt **dissolves**. It breaks up into pieces so tiny that you can't see them any more. These tiny pieces spread through the water. This special type of mixture is called a **solution**.

If you tasted the solution, it would taste salty. A less yucky way to prove the salt is there is to pop a fresh egg into the jar before adding the salt. In fresh water, the egg sinks, but a solution with lots of salt in is **denser**, so the egg floats!

SEE THE SCIENCE ⬎

Mix these materials with water to find out which ones are **soluble** (dissolve) in water and which ones are **insoluble** (don't dissolve) in water: salt, sugar, coffee granules, milk, gravy granules, baking soda, vitamin C tablets, dishwashing liquid, squash, cooking oil

Do not taste or eat any of your mixtures, and pour them out afterwards so that no one else drinks them by mistake!

Dissolving Detective

Can water keep **dissolving** a substance forever? Does the temperature of the water make a difference? Try these **experiments** to find out.

How Many Sugars?

Equipment

- Salt
- Sugar
- Baking soda
- Water from a cold tap
- Three jars (or glasses)
- Dark paper
- Measuring jugs
- Teaspoon
- Spoon for stirring

Method

1 Measure half a jug of water into each jar. Place them on a dark surface. This will help you to see if the substances have dissolved.

2 Measure salt into the first jar, a teaspoon at a time. Stir after adding each teaspoon. Does the salt dissolve?

3 Keep adding salt to the same jar, a teaspoon at a time. How many teaspoons can you add before it stops dissolving?

If you can see tiny specks of salt that don't dissolve after stirring, the water has dissolved as much salt as it can.

Predict: Will you be able to dissolve the same amount, more, or less of the other substances in the same amount of water?

4 Repeat with the other jars using sugar and baking soda. How many teaspoons can you add before they stop dissolving?

IS IT A FAIR TEST?

The **variable** you are changing is the **material** being dissolved. Make sure the volume and temperature of the water are the same in every jar. You'll find out why this is important in the next experiment!

Material	Teaspoons added before it stopped dissolving
Salt	
Sugar	
Baking soda	

Record your results in a table like this.

5 **Analyze** your results. Was there a difference?

Find the Solution

Does the temperature of the water change the amount of salt that **dissolves**? Carry out a second **experiment** to find out.

Equipment

- Salt
- Cold water
- Hot water
- Two jars or glasses
- Measuring jug

- Teaspoon
- Spoon for stirring

Method

1 Measure half a jug of water from the cold tap into one jar and half a jug of water from the hot tap into the second jar.

Predict: Will warmer water dissolve more or less salt?

ADULT HELP

Ask an adult to check the water is not too hot before you use the tap.

2 Measure salt into the first jar a teaspoon at a time. Stir after each spoonful. How many teaspoons can you add before the salt stops dissolving?

3 Measure salt into the jar of warm water a teaspoon at a time. Stir after adding each teaspoon. How many teaspoons can you add before the salt stops dissolving?

4 **Analyze** your results. Did changing the temperature make a difference?

REAL WORLD SCIENCE

People heat water to make solutions such as coffee, tea, gravy, and hot chocolate. The hot water helps the substances dissolve more quickly.

Conclusion

Some **materials** are **soluble** in water. This is a **property** of these materials. However, there is a limit to how much can dissolve. This is different for different materials. It also changes with the temperature of the water. When the water has dissolved all the material it can, we say the **solution** is saturated.

How Can Mixtures Be Separated?

You can always separate a **mixture** and get the original **materials** back. Mixing is **reversible**. Knowing the **properties** of each material in a mixture helps us work out how to separate them.

Separating Solids

You could separate a mixture of candies by picking out all the green ones. It would not be so easy to separate a mixture of flour and rice by hand, but you could **sieve** the mixture. Tiny pieces of flour pass through the sieve. Larger rice grains are left behind.

Combine harvesters have sieves inside. The part of the crop we want—the tiny grains—fall through the holes and are collected. The bits we can't eat are left behind and dropped back on to the field.

The best way to separate a mixture depends on the properties of the materials. Garbage trucks deliver a mixture of many different materials to recycling centers. Some of these materials are separated by hand. Blasts of air separate paper and cardboard from heavier materials. Magnets are used to separate steel and aluminium cans.

Separating Solids and Liquids

What about a **mixture** of sand and water? You could filter the mixture. The tiny holes in filter paper let water through but trap sand or soil.

Separating Solutions

Sieving and filtering will not help you to separate **solutions**. The **dissolved** salt and the water can both pass through tiny holes. Instead, you can heat the water until it evaporates (turns into a gas and goes into the air). The salt will be left behind. The **water vapor** can be caught and cooled, so it changes back into water.

SEE THE SCIENCE ⬇

Fizzy drinks have a gas dissolved in them. The gas usually separates from the liquid slowly and escapes as tiny bubbles. You can speed this up by dropping a sugar cube into a bottle of fizzy drink. Bubbles of gas form quickly on the rough surface.

 Place the bottle in a sink or in the lawn when you do this!

Separating Mixtures

Chromatography is another clever way to separate solutions. You can use it to investigate the mixtures of colors used to make brown candys.

Equipment

- Large square of white filter paper, blotting paper, or art paper
- Different brands of candy with brown sugar shells
- Drinking straw
- Glass of water

Method

1. Put the square of paper on a flat, waterproof surface. Arrange the candy evenly across the center of the paper.

   Write down the names of all the candy so that you know which is which.

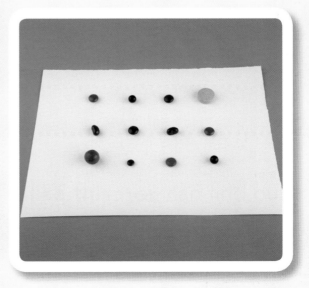

2 Use the straw to put six drops of water on each candy.

📋 IS IT A FAIR TEST?

The **variable** you are changing is the type of candy. Everything else should stay the same. Add the same amount of water to each candy, and leave it for the same amount of time. Is it a fair test if each candy is a different size and shape? How could you make your **experiment** fairer?

3 The drops of water should form a pool underneath each candy. Leave your experiment for 5 to 10 minutes.

4 Look at the paper around each candy. What do you see? Let the paper dry out. Draw a table to record your results.

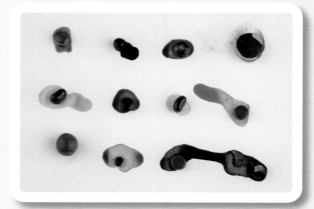

Brand of candy	Colors on paper after chromatography
M&Ms	
Reeses Pieces	
Skittles	

5 **Analyze** your results. Did each brown candy produce the same number of colors? Is there a difference between candy made with artificial colors and candy marked "no artificial colors?"

Conclusion

All dyes and colorings are a **mixture** of the primary colours—blue, yellow, and red. Each dye is a different **material**. In this experiment, the brown coloring from different candies **dissolved** in water.
The **solution** traveled through the paper. The water could carry some colors farther than others, so the colors were separated. This shows that "brown" is made up in many different ways.

The most **soluble** dyes are usually carried the farthest. Try the same experiment using different colored candy.

Changed Forever

Scientists love mixing **materials** together to find out what happens. Some materials may form a **mixture** or a **solution**. Others **react** together to make completely new materials.

SEE THE SCIENCE ⬇

Add a teaspoon of baking soda to water—it **dissolves** and forms a solution. Now add a teaspoon of baking soda to vinegar. What signs are there that the soda and vinegar are changing into new materials?

One of the new materials is a gas. You can collect it inside a balloon!

Heating Mixtures

Some **irreversible** changes happen only when you add heat. A mixture of paper and air does nothing. But if you add heat, the paper and air burn. They change into ash and gases. Burning is an irreversible change.

Baking is also an irreversible change. You can't change a cake back into flour, sugar, butter, and eggs once it has been cooked.

Irreversible changes can be very useful. When a material burns, lots of energy is released. We use the energy from burning fuel to heat and light our homes and to power machines.

SEE THE SCIENCE ⬇

Some changes, or **reactions**, happen very quickly. Others are much slower. Leave an iron nail outside for a few days. The iron reacts with air and water and changes into rust. The rust is a new material. You can scrape it off, but you can't separate it back into iron, water, and air.

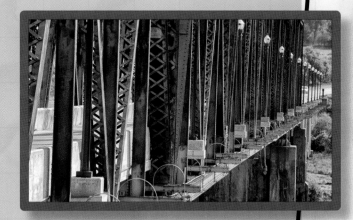

Sometimes we look for ways to stop or slow down changes. We paint iron to stop it from rusting, and we keep food in the fridge to slow down **decay**.

Plastic From a Cow?

Irreversible changes can help scientists to make new **materials** with different **properties**. **Experiment** with vinegar and milk to design a new material of your own.

Equipment

- ½ bottle each of four different types of milk (such as whole milk, 2% milk, skim milk, soy milk, or rice milk)
- Jug
- White vinegar
- Small pan and heat source
- Spoon
- Sieve
- Wet wipes

Method

ADULT HELP

1. Ask an adult to heat half a bottle of whole milk gently. When the milk is warm (but not boiling), ask the adult to pour it into a jug.

2 Add two teaspoons of vinegar to the milk in the jug. Stir gently. What happens? Can you see any signs that the materials are changing?

3 After a minute, pour the contents of the jug through the sieve. What can you see in the sieve?

> Place a wet wipe over the base of the sieve. This will make the next step easier.

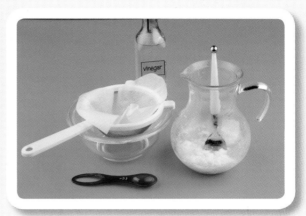

4 When the lumps are cool, gather the cloth and twist gently to squeeze out any remaining liquid.

5 Open up the cloth—you have made a ball of white material. How does it look, feel, and smell? What happens when you squeeze it, shape it, or bounce it? Record your **observations**.

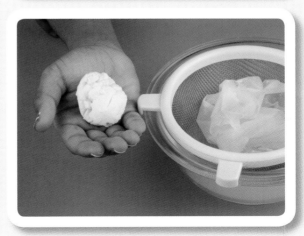

What Happened?

When you mix together vinegar and warm milk, the **materials react** and change. A new material forms, called a polymer (like plastic).

6 Repeat steps 1 to 5 using a different type of milk each time.

> Put each plastic in a different container, labeled with the type of milk you used.

7 Leave the lumps to dry overnight, then try squeezing and bouncing them. How do they look, feel, and behave now? Record your **observations** at each stage. Use a table like the one below, so it is easy to compare your results when the **experiment** is over.

Type of milk	Observations at stage 5	Observations at stage 7
Whole milk		
2% milk		
Skim milk		
Soy milk		

Predict: Will different milks produce different plastics, or will they all be the same?

IS IT A FAIR TEST?

You should only change one **variable** at a time—the type of milk. The amount of milk and vinegar should stay the same. Is it a fair test if the milk is heated to a different temperature each time? How could you make your experiment fairer?

8 **Analyze** your results. Were your predictions right?

Conclusion

Milk is full of protein. Adding vinegar causes the protein to stick together in long chains. These chains clump together, catching the fat in the milk like fish in a net. Different types of milk have different amounts of fat and protein in them. This is why they form "plastics" with different **properties**.

Don't taste or eat any of the materials used or formed in your experiments. Remember to wash your hands after touching home-made polymers.

Your polymer will become very hard. Shape it while soft, then paint and varnish it once it has dried out.

Plan Your Next Experiment

Experiments have helped you discover some amazing things about **materials**. Just like you, scientists carry out experiments to answer questions and test ideas. Each experiment is planned carefully to make it a fair test.

Scientists are finding out new facts all the time. Experiments also lead to new questions!

Did you think of more questions about materials? Can you plan new experiments to help answer them?

Being a scientist and carrying out experiments is exciting. What will you discover next?

YOU FOUND OUT THAT...

Materials have different physical **properties**, which make them suitable for different jobs.

Some materials can be mixed together. Others don't mix. Some materials form a **solution** when they are mixed. There is a limit to how much material can **dissolve** in a certain amount of water.

Mixtures can always be separated. Some are easier to separate then others. You can work out how to separate a mixture by thinking about the properties of the different materials in the mixture.

Materials have different chemical properties. If two materials **react** together, they are changed forever. The change is **irreversible**. This can be very useful when we want to create new materials.

WHAT NEXT?

Can you design an experiment to test how waterproof or stretchy different materials are?

Oil does not dissolve in water. but if you shake them together, they form a mixture called an emulsion. Plan an experiment to find out if adding salt or pepper to salad dressing helps this emulsion to stay mixed.

Experiment to find the best method of separating a mixture of salt and sand. Hint: Like in the Separating Mixtures chromatography experiment, you will need to make a solution first!

There are other materials that have similar **properties** to vinegar. Scientists call these acids. Plan an experiment to find out if different types of acid (for example, lemon juice) make different milk plastics.

Glossary

analyze examine the results of an experiment carefully in order to explain what happened

decay reactions that break down a living thing after it has died

density how heavy an object is for its size

dissolve become broken up into tiny pieces and spread through a liquid

experiment procedure carried out to test an idea or answer a question

insoluble does not dissolve (in a particular liquid)

irreversible can't be reversed or undone

material what something is made of

mixture substance made by mixing materials together

observation noting or measuring what you see, hear, smell, or feel

opaque does not let light pass through

prediction best guess or estimate of what will happen, based on what you already know

properties how a material looks or behaves

react change

reaction when two or more materials have an effect on each other that causes them to change

reversible can be reversed or undone

scientific inquiry method used by scientists to answer questions about the world

sieve put a substance or material through a mesh strainer, which separates coarse and fine particles

soluble dissolves (in a particular liquid)

solution mixture of a liquid and another substance, which has dissolved in the liquid

synthetic human-made

transparent lets light pass through; see-through

variable something that can be changed during an experiment

water vapor water that has changed into a gas

Find out more

Books

Challoner, Jack and Maggie Hewson. *Hands-On Science: Matter and Materials*. New York: Kingfisher Publishing, 2013.

Oxlade, Chris. *Experiments with Matter and Materials*. Excellent Science Experiments. New York: PowerKids Press, 2015.

Spilsbury, Richard and Louise Spilsbury. *Materials*. Essential Physical Science. Chicago: Capstone Heinemann Library, 2014.

Websites

FactHound offers a safe, fun way to find Internet sites related to this book. All of the sites on FactHound have been researched by our staff.

Here's all you do:

Visit *www.facthound.com*

Type in this code: 9781410979230

Index